HEAD FIRST
Portraits from the Arts Council Collection

Arts Council Collection

Published on the occasion of *Head First: Portraits from the Arts Council Collection*, an Arts Council Collection exhibition toured by National Touring Exhibitions from the Hayward Gallery, London, for the Arts Council of England

Exhibition tour:

City Gallery, Leicester	17 January – 28 February 1998
City Art Gallery, Southampton	9 April – 31 May
Abbot Hall Art Gallery, Kendal	10 June – 13 September
Hatton Gallery, University of Newcastle	26 September – 8 November
Victoria Art Gallery, Bath	16 January – 28 February 1999
Graves Art Gallery, Sheffield	6 March – 18 April
Ferens Art Gallery, Kingston upon Hull	April – June

Exhibition selected by Richard Shone
Exhibition organised by Vicki Lewis, assisted by Katrina Crookall

Catalogue designed by Jason Ellams
Printed by The Beacon Press, UK

709. 4092 ART

Front cover: Michael Andrews, *Study of a head for a group of figures No. 6*, 1967, © Estate of the artist 1998

Back cover: Gilbert & George, Still from *A Portrait of The Artists as Young Men*, 1972, © the artists 1998

Photographs: Bridgeman Art Library, London (pp. 23, 37, 85); Marcus Leith (pp. 21, 27, 29, 41, 43, 51, 65, 67, 71, 75, 77, 87); John Webb (pp. 17, 19, 53, 57, 61, 63); Stephen White (p. 5)

© The South Bank Centre 1998
Essay © Richard Shone 1998

Arts Council Collection, Hayward Gallery and National Touring Exhibitions publications are distributed by Cornerhouse Publications, 70 Oxford Street, Manchester M1 5NH (tel. 0161 237 9662; fax. 0161 237 9664).

For further information about works in the Arts Council Collection, please write to Isobel Johnstone, Curator of the Arts Council Collection, Hayward Gallery, SBC, Royal Festival Hall, London SE1 8XX.

THE SURREY INSTITUTE OF ART & DESIGN

Farnham Campus, Falkner Road, Farnham, Surrey GU9 7DS

PREFACE

The Arts Council Collection is the largest national loan collection of post-war British art. Its works are lent on a temporary basis to exhibitions and longer-term to museums and public buildings throughout the country. The Collection also plays an integral role in National Touring Exhibitions which annually shows up to 30 exhibitions at 160 venues to 1.4 million people. Both the Collection and National Touring Exhibitions are managed by the Hayward Gallery on behalf of the Arts Council of England.

The Arts Council Collection is a unique national resource and can lend works to an extent impossible for other national collections. At the time of its founding as part of the Council for the Encouragement of Music and Arts in 1942, it focused on buying historical twentieth-century works; in recent decades, it has concentrated on buying work from living artists. The Collection is rich and diverse; in spite of some pre-war gaps, it reflects most shifts in taste and patronage since the war.

For *Head First: Portraits from the Arts Council Collection* we have had the fortunate opportunity to add works from city and regional galleries and museums who are participating in its tour, thus allowing a fuller exploration of twentieth-century portraiture, and reflecting the development of the genre in an ever-changing society. By drawing on treasures from other collections, *Head First* will change in form and context as it travels.

Our greatest thanks are due to Richard Shone for his selection of *Head First* and the insights he has brought to it. His unfailing good humour has also made the creation of the show a pleasure.

In addition to those artists who have kindly provided information and support, we warmly thank the following lenders for their generosity and invaluable cooperation: Abbot Hall Art Gallery, Kendal; Ferens Art Gallery, Kingston upon Hull; Hatton Gallery, University of Newcastle; New Walk Museum, Leicester City Museums; Sheffield City Art Galleries; Southampton City Art Gallery; and Victoria Art Gallery, Bath & North East Somerset.

We are also extremely grateful to our collaborators on the project: Adrienne Avery-Gray, Christian Barnes, Jon Benington, Ann Bukantas, Anne Goodchild, David Jackson, Edward King, Martyn Ladds, David Scruton, Stephen Snoddy and Sylvia Wright.

Susan Ferleger Brades
Director, Hayward Gallery

Vicki Lewis
Exhibition Organiser

HEAD FIRST
Richard Shone

Without portraiture, British art is almost unimaginable. Next to landscape, it is the one arena in which British painters and sculptors have excelled. From the Elizabethan miniaturists through to our own times, it has run with hardly a break, drawing into its web nearly all the great names in painting and sculpture. In the past, portraiture was the chief occupation of most of the foreign artists who worked in Britain. It dominated the eighteenth century and, in recent years, has exercised, albeit in surprising and less familiar ways, a variety of prominent figures. The portraits chosen for *Head First* encompass a great range of approach and style, of media employed and sitters represented.

In the twentieth century, portraits have frequently been controversial, especially when the work in question is of a well-known person commissioned by a public body or, as often with sculpture, for a public place. The succession of rows over portraits by Jacob Epstein, Augustus John, Walter Sickert and Graham Sutherland has enlivened the social history of modern British art. This continuing emotive power was conclusively demonstrated by three front-page events in September 1997. There was the display of Marcus Harvey's *Myra* at the Royal Academy of Arts' exhibition *Sensation* which led to immediate uproar and swift vandalisation. Shortly before *Myra* went on view, there was press criticism over the commissioned portrait of John Major by John Wonnacott when it was unveiled at the National Portrait Gallery. And thirdly, the public mourning of Diana, Princess of Wales, brought sharply to the fore the power of the human image – formal and informal photographic portraits of the Princess were inescapable during the weeks following her death.

Marcus Harvey
Myra, 1995
acrylic on canvas
The Saatchi Collection, London
© the artist 1998. Courtesy of Jay Jopling

Harvey's painting is a substantial image of Myra Hindley based on a notorious police photograph of the Moors murderer. The painting's source is instantly recognizable and horribly familiar. What then were the reasons behind the outcry? It is not a straight portrait of Hindley: she did not sit for the artist. Nor is it a faithful reproduction of the photograph. It was built up from innumerable 'prints' of the cast of a child's hand in much the same way as Ben Day dots form a newspaper photo. It is, then, a portrait not of Hindley exactly, but of an icon, a representation of Hindley which has come to stand for unadulterated evil. It provokes fears of murder and paedophilia and abhorrence at Hindley's specific crimes. The undisguised sensual component of the image of Hindley is unavoidable, especially on the large scale of this painting – it was after all a young woman who had committed such monstrous crimes. Her sex has bestowed on her a prominence in the criminal pantheon far outweighing that of Brady, who actually committed the murders.

A fundamental iconoclasm runs deep in human nature and the 'portrait' is frequently a victim. We tear up photos of ex-lovers, defile images of people we dislike, destroy statues to deposed tyrants and politicians, remove portraits of men and women who have lost whatever eminence they once had. In recent decades defilement of works of contemporary art of all kinds has increased and it is surely significant that the two men who, separately, attacked *Myra*, supposedly on moral grounds, were reported as being artists, adding another element to the multi-layered reactions to the work.

John Wonnacott
John Major, 1997
oil on board
Courtesy of the National Portrait
Gallery, London

In the case of Wonnacott's portrait of John Major the abuse it received was more distinctly of two kinds – aesthetic and personal. The pose was deemed untypical, the setting inappropriate and parts of the painting incoherent. Major looked too tired; Mrs Major, in the background, too small. In 1984, Rodrigo Moynihan's portrait of Major's predecessor, Margaret Thatcher, another commission from the National Portrait Gallery, was similarly criticized for its grand setting (also 10 Downing Street) and for the fact that the sitter seemed to be squinting. Complaints led to Moynihan having to return to the work after it had gone on show at the National Portrait Gallery to 'repair the damage' of public criticism. At the time of writing, Wonnacott's painting remains unchanged.

In the same month, photographs of Diana, Princess of Wales, at all ages and in all moods, were showered across newspapers and magazines, flashed on television, stuck on to shop windows, festooned along royal railings and made the centrepiece of improvised, candlelit altars. They formed a shifting collective portrait which was summarized by an enormous head of the Princess carried out in coloured chalks on a London pavement by a lone street artist.

All three images – Myra Hindley, John Major and Diana, Princess of Wales – represent in the public's mind three overwhelming ingredients of public life: crime, politics and royalty. In their contrasting ways, all are public pictorial signs and as such are easily recognized, even though reactions to them are highly complex. This iconic and symbolic role of portraiture has been the strongest contributory element to its survival.

For centuries in Britain, making portraits has been an industry for its painters and sculptors and, more recently, its photographers. The national school could hardly have developed without a public's insatiable desire to be recorded. Supply met demand. Foreign artists working in Britain in the sixteenth and seventeenth centuries were predominantly portraitists – from Hans Holbein and Marcus Gheeraerts through Daniel Mytens, Anthony van Dyck, Peter Lely and Godfrey Kneller, to J.M. Rysbrack and François Roubiliac in the eighteenth century. Other genres such as landscape were developed later; only religious art preceded portraiture as an accepted form of visual expression. The presence of foreign portraitists inevitably sharpened the competitive instincts of native practitioners. However, the example of Holbein's portraiture, for instance, scarcely entered the mainstream and his strongest influence is seen in the development of the portrait miniature (a technique learnt by Holbein when he was in England). It was left to William Hogarth in the early eighteenth century to democratize the English portrait, wresting it from a near monopoly of aristocratic patronage.

The social advancement and financial gain to be had from the practice of portraiture may have overwhelmed many a precarious talent (and even a talent as spectacular, for example, as John Everett Millais) but it was undertaken, at one stage or another, by nearly all the prominent names in British art – John Constable making the most surprising contribution to the genre (next, perhaps, to J.M.W. Turner's youthful *Self Portrait*, c.1798, in the Tate Gallery). Although portraiture helped artists to pay the bills and support other, more sympathetic, activities, its constant demands could generate extreme frustration. Thomas Gainsborough longed to abandon his portrait factory in Pall Mall in order to paint landscapes. John Singer Sargent more or less gave up painted portraiture for the last twenty or so years of his life. During that same period (c.1905–25), Augustus John became the best-known 'modern' portraitist in Britain although he too preferred landscape and figure compositions. It is frequently assumed that a continual stream of sitters de-vitalized him and ruined his gifts. But it seems doubtful whether he would have succeeded in any other mode as resoundingly as he did in a handful of his portraits. John's genuine longing to give up commissioned portraits, however, was an all too familiar if temporary *cri de coeur* among such portraitists as William Orpen, Ambrose McEvoy and John Lavery. Walter Richard Sickert, on the other hand, was completely mercenary and only resorted to commissioned portraits when his creditors became too pressing; most of his best portraits are of models such as the young Belgian woman in *Head of a Woman*, 1906 (cat. 1). Even established portrait photographers have left behind in their studios evidence of their frustrated longing to snap landscape, streets, interiors, anything, in fact, but the single figure with its greedy claims upon their lens and time.

As the twentieth century has progressed, it has become increasingly difficult to square the demands of portraiture with those of being a consciously 'modern' artist. Most of the leading movements of the century have been stylistically inimical to the vivid realization of human beings. Of course, great and good portraits have been painted but the achievement of the work as painting is nearly always superior to it as portrait. Picasso's celebrated image of Gertrude Stein (1905–06; The Metropolitan Museum of Art, New York) is one of the last great collaborations between painter and subject, the result of eighty sittings. With many artists the element of portraiture, of getting the image 'like', has been a secondary consideration; the realization of a human head or figure, uncompromised by the exigencies of capturing a likeness, has been the artist's chief object. Francis Bacon's free interpretations of the faces of his friends or Frank Auerbach's series of paintings of his constant sitters (cat. 38) reveal more about the artist than the model.

In *Head First* the majority of the figures portrayed are either from the artist's immediate family (Victor Pasmore's wife, Vanessa Bell's daughter, David Hockney's father) or circle of friends (Henri Gaudier-Brzeska of

Horace Brodzky, Anthony Devas of Rupert Shephard, Howard Hodgkin of Jane Kasmin). Here the artist can take liberties and use a model for ends rather different from 'straight' portraiture. Hockney's image of his father is an outstanding example, a cautionary tale in which he pits modernist devices against the figure of a loved parent (cat. 39). Devas' casual, domestic image – superior to many of his commissioned portraits for which he was well known – shows his fellow artist, Rupert Shephard (who was later to marry Devas' widow Nicolette), listening in to the wireless for war-time news bulletins, a ritual carried out across the country (cat. 24). The picture was briefly famous for its encapsulation of the national mood but in Devas' circle it was not much liked and Shephard's future wife took against its prosaic portrayal of her fiancé. Again, Josef Herman's head-and-shoulders portrait of a Welsh miner was drawn from a man who worked in the mining village where Herman lived for several years; but the generalized, bullish figure becomes a symbol of hard manual work (cat. 31). Another symbolic image, Nigel Henderson's grim photographic collage *Head of a Man*, 1956–61 (cat. 35), is related to Henderson's contri-bution to the famous environmental exhibition *This is Tomorrow* held at the Whitechapel Art Gallery in 1956. The head was intended to symbolize the thinking process that man brings to bear on his natural surroundings. The visor-like forehead was produced by the superimposition of a photo of a bronze shoe on a photo of the man's collaged face, and the heavily-textured skin was meant to suggest hide or bark to further the image's association with nature. The complex evolution and specific context of the work produced a sinister, acutely-realized but anonymous portrait. *Hugh Gaitskell as a Famous Monster of Filmland*, 1964 (cat. 37), by Henderson's colleague and friend Richard Hamilton, shares technical similarities with Henderson's work as well as the looming closeness of the image to the picture plane. The head is a satirical composite of the then Leader of the Labour Party Hugh Gaitskell (1906–63) and of the film actor Claude Rains made up as the Phantom of the Opera. Although Hamilton's politics were to the Left, he greatly disapproved of what seemed to him Gaitskell's lacklustre leadership and refusal to form an anti-nuclear policy for adoption by his Party. The result is both biting and luridly comic as well as being instantly recognizable to anyone familiar with the politician's face. Hamilton has combined public portraiture with sharp personal criticism in an image that directly descends from the great caricaturists such as Thomas Rowlandson, James Gillray and George Cruikshank.

The only commissioned work in *Head First* is Frank Dobson's sculpture of the great Russian dancer Lydia Lopokova, an entirely successful work in which artist, sitter and patron appear to have been highly satisfied with the result (cat. 13). In 1923, the economist John Maynard Keynes (later the first Chairman of the Arts Council of Great Britain), who was in love with Lopokova (they married two years later), commissioned Dobson to make a bust of the diminutive, high-spirited dancer. The sittings in the sculptor's London studio were congenial; Lopokova is caught in characteristic pose as though airily talking at the table on which she rests her elbows. The well-to-do Keynes was not put out by the comparatively hefty price of about £160 which Dobson asked. At the same time it was generally recognized that with this work Dobson had reached a new level of maturity as an artist.

At the other end of the spectrum from the contractual complexities of commissioned portraiture are self-portraits. Although they may of course come about through a commission (for example, for the collection of artists' self-portraits in the Uffizi), self-portraits are invariably carried out at the artist's own whim. They have no one but themselves to satisfy and can interpret and take liberties at will. For this reason they can be extremely revealing or unusual (or even misleading) and appear to have tempted even those artists for whom portraiture was never a chief concern – Constable and Turner, of course, but also Samuel Palmer, Richard Parkes Bonington and, in our own century, Edward Wadsworth, Barbara Hepworth and Richard Hamilton. *Head First* contains both traditional and unexpected examples of self-portraiture. Mark Gertler shows himself at the age of 29, about to begin the most successful decade of his career: his assumed hauteur and pleasure in his own looks do not entirely conceal a note of watchful apprehension (cat. 10). The fine pencil drawing by Stanley Spencer, his head seen from slightly below, contains wariness and concentration in the swift mapping of his features (cat. 16). Variations on the self-portrait occur in two much later works. In Gilbert & George's

Maurice Beck and Helen Macgregor
Mr and Mrs Maynard Keynes, 1925
black and white photograph
photograph © Condé Nast
Publications Ltd/British Vogue

video *A Portrait of the Artists as Young Men*, 1972 (cat. 43), Gilbert (on the right) and George (on the left) slowly turn their heads, revealing different angles in the sharp photographic light in which they were filmed, accompanied by a soundtrack of thunder and rain. Already in this early film, the artists' studied formality and grave demeanour announce their reiterated double-presence in so many of their later works. They are, as suggested in the title, both onlookers to and participants in the extra-ordinary human scene which they have continued to explore throughout their work, to which the face and human figure is central. Michael Craig-Martin's *Kid's Stuff 1-7*, 1973 (cat. 44), in which the spectator is reflected in a series of small mirrors, each one accompanied by a hand-written, self-questioning statement (for example, 'How strange it is to be my present age'), obviously began as a self-portrait, for the artist himself was the viewer as the work was being made. Placed on show, the spectator becomes the 'subject' in the mirrors and, by considering the texts and the reactions they evoke, he or she builds up a momentary self-portrait. Such ambiguity – do we feel the way we look, look the way we feel? – is at the heart of much of Craig-Martin's work, sounding a note of personal anxiety which, in *Kid's Stuff*, the viewer can scarcely avoid.

Images such as these raise some fundamental questions about portraiture. What, for example, do we expect of a 'likeness'? How important is it to the viewer to feel that the portrait really does resemble its subject? Max Beerbohm used to complain that so few people looked like themselves, wittily putting his finger on the changeability of human expression. An artist's satisfaction with the likeness produced may well be at odds with the sitter's feelings or with the sometimes even stronger reactions of the sitter's family or friends. We have only to remember Lady Churchill's violent reaction to Graham Sutherland's portrait of her husband which other judges felt was extraordinarily like Churchill: she hated it so much that she destroyed it. Was Sutherland's portrayal too faithful or did she feel he had missed some essential ingredient in Churchill's character (which perhaps only she could recognize) or was the work too 'modern' for her taste? Again, when Sutherland made his celebrated portrait of the writer Somerset Maugham, Maugham's long-standing friend Sir Gerald Kelly P.R.A. wrote amusingly of it: 'To think that I have known [Maugham] since 1902 and have only just recognized that, disguised as an old Chinese Madame, he kept a Brothel in Shanghai!'. Sutherland had captured a startling aspect of Maugham's physical appearance that had previously gone unnoticed or was thought unmentionable. In this sense the likeness is a 'faithful' one and such faithfulness is certainly the chief requirement of a portrait. But, looking at Gaudier-Brzeska's forceful drawing of his friend and fellow-artist, Horace Brodzky, it is clear that conscious distortion of the features for stylistic truth has resulted in a potent sense of individual character and physique (cat. 7). This surely applies to every 'head' that Francis Bacon undertook (cat. 32). Again, the distortion apparent in the photographic source of Richard Hamilton's image of Derek Jarman produces a haunting, even alarming portrait of the painter and film maker shortly before he died from AIDS, the word itself discernible on the canvas behind Jarman's head (cat. 54).

Many portraits may fulfil the requirements of accuracy but fail to convey anything about the sitter beyond physical resemblance. This raises the troubling question of how much a portrait can indeed reveal about a person's individual psychology. It is relatively easy to suggest a sitter's profession or occupation, social standing or temporary circumstances (through clothes, props and setting). But what can we tell from a portrait beyond fairly general characteristics – seriousness, meanness, forthrightness, sex-appeal, reserve? There has always been a dangerous tendency to follow Arthur Schopenhauer's classic statement that a man's face is far more revealing than his talk 'for it is the compendium of all which he will ever say as it is the register of all his thoughts and aspirations'. Who knows if Frans Hals' jolly cavalier was not, in reality, an arrogant bully by nature or that Titian's young man with a tattered glove – an image of other-worldly

Henri Gaudier-Brzeska
Horace Brodzky, 1913
bronze (posthumous cast)
Tate Gallery, London

contemplation – was not a foolish artist's model, vain of his looks and longing for a glass of local red? Further complicating this question of the revelation of character is our knowledge of the sitter when he or she is named and known – a famous writer, scientist or general, for example. Here, we bring our own impressions and facts to a reading of the face just as the artist may well have used their own knowledge of the sitter's achievements and personality in delineating his or her features (sometimes making them more interesting to look at than they are). I think it is safe to say that a good or conscientious artist will not stray too far from the essence of the sitter's character but that subtle readings based on a physical image are at best dubious. In *Head First* we are confronted more by telling or affecting moods than by acute analyses of character. And in one or two cases we have nothing to go on beyond a purely physical impression, as in Michael Andrews' study of a man's head taken from a large, group photograph (cat. 41). And as we know, the photograph often lies.

A picture of a person – whether one of considerable aesthetic achievement or a smiling snap in a family album – is essentially a memento, a souvenir, the result of a desire, as John Brophy wrote in his book *The Human Face*, 'to outwit the oblivion of death'. It shows we exist, that we are not nonentities, that we have not passed through the world without leaving a trace of ourselves. At the same time, as Henry James noted in a passage in *The Tragic Muse*, portraiture is one of the most valuable ways in which the past has been documented, opening windows into history and psychology. In scrutinising images of other people, their gestures and expressions, how time has affected them, which foot they have put forward for us to see, we are indeed looking at ourselves, often more closely than we might like.

Further Reading

Anthony Bertram, *English Portraiture*, London, 1924

Richard Brilliant, *Portraiture*, London, 1991

John Brophy, *The Human Face*, London, 1945

Robin Gibson, *The Portrait Now*, National Portrait Gallery, London, 1993

Allan Gwynne-Jones, *Portrait Painters*, London, 1950

John Hayes, *The Portrait in British Art*, National Portrait Gallery, London, 1991

Ian G. Lumsden, *From Sickert to Dalí: International Portraits*, Beaverbrook Art Gallery, New Brunswick, exhibition catalogue, 1976

Christopher Newall and Stanley Olsen, *Society Portraits 1850–1939*, Clarendon Gallery, London, exhibition catalogue, 1985

Picturing People. British Figurative Art Since 1945, British Council, exhibition catalogue, 1989–90

Marcia Pointon, *Hanging the Head*, London and New Haven, 1993

John Russell, *British Portrait Painters*, London, 1944

Robin Simon, *The Portrait in Britain and America*, Oxford, 1987

Monroe Wheeler, *20th Century Portraits*, Museum of Modern Art, New York, exhibition catalogue, 1942

PLATES

Catalogue numbers: The works, comprising those illustrated as Plates and those not illustrated (listed at the back), are numbered chronologically in a single sequence.

Note: All measurements are given as height x width x depth unless stated otherwise.

Walter Richard Sickert (1860–1942)

1
Head of a Woman, 1906
(also known as *The Belgian Cocotte*)
oil on canvas
49.3 x 39.3 cm
Arts Council Collection

The sitter is Jeanne Daurmont who, with her sister Hélène, modelled
for several paintings by the artist in spring 1906 (including *The Belgian
Cocottes*, Portsmouth City Museum). Sickert met Jeanne (a milliner) and
Hélène (a charwoman) in Soho when he heard them asking a policeman, in
French, where they could buy coffee. In earlier years Sickert's best portraits
are informal, usually of models or casual acquaintances. In his later years he
painted portraits mainly from photographs or small preliminary drawings.
Head of a Woman is one of the most spontaneous and vivid portrait heads
from his Camden Town period (though the work was in fact painted in his
studio at 8 Fitzroy Street).

Gwen John (1876–1939)

4
Bust of a Girl with a Bow before a Pink Background, undated
(probably 1910–20)
oil on canvas
23 x 13.7 cm
Arts Council Collection

Like her younger brother Augustus, Gwen John first studied at the Slade
School of Art. From 1898 she continued her studies in Paris for two years at
the Académie Carmen where Whistler taught. When she was twenty-seven
she moved to France permanently, leading a mostly solitary existence.
She painted mainly portraits of women, girls in church, her cats and an
occasional interior. After 1910 her pictures showed a restricted tonal range,
with colours limited to greys and pinks. In 1914 she moved to the village
of Meudon on the outskirts of Paris, where she lived until her death. Near
her home was an order of nuns, some of whom she painted. The nuns
had orphan girls in their care and *Bust of a Girl with a Bow before a Pink
Background* may be a portrait of one of them.

Henri Gaudier-Brzeska (1891–1915)

7
Portrait of Horace Brodzky, 1913
pastel on paper
25.4 x 21 cm
Arts Council Collection

This work was made in 1913, the year in which the young French artist
Gaudier-Brzeska met Brodzky, a painter, illustrator and engraver. Brodzky
was American but born in Melbourne, Australia, in 1885. He studied there
and in London, where he became a member of the London Group. He was
a prolific printmaker, and in 1933 published a book about Gaudier-Brzeska.

In a later publication, *Gaudier-Brzeska Drawings* (1946), Brodzky wrote:
'His pastels, very few in number, were usually done in strongly contrasted
colours, something no doubt evolved from Gauguin, from Les Fauves and
the Cubists in Paris. These pastels consist of a few portraits and still-life
subjects ... In his lineal drawings, in which he often relies upon a contour
for effect, Gaudier-Brzeska is more himself and at his best.'

Roger Fry (1866–1934)

8
Portrait of Edith Sitwell, 1915
oil on canvas
61 x 46 cm
Sheffield City Art Galleries

Like her brothers Sir Osbert and Sacheverell Sitwell, Dame Edith Sitwell (1887–1964) was a poet, critic and biographer, her poetry perhaps the most enduring of this celebrated literary trio's prolific output. A miscellany called *Wheels* (1916–21), funded by herself, her brothers and her friends, helped to make her work more widely known. Her *Collected Poems* were issued in 1930.

This painting was carried out in Roger Fry's London studio in Fitzroy Street, the sitter wearing a long green evening dress which, as she remembered years later, caused considerable mirth among the children of the district when she walked at midday, accompanied by Fry in a sombrero, from his studio for lunch nearby. Compared to her appearance in later years, however, the poet is chastely unadorned in Fry's painting.

Jacob Epstein (1880–1959)

9
Mrs Epstein (Margaret Dunlop), 1918
bronze
39 x 44 x 31 cm
New Walk Museum, Leicester City Museums
© Estate of the artist 1998
Shown at City Gallery, Leicester, only

This is the third and finest of three portraits which the artist made of his
first wife Margaret Dunlop. He said: 'This bust, I think, is the most profound
of the three works, and it has that quiet thoughtfulness that I had uncon-
sciously striven for in the other two; or most likely, as I matured in my work, I
naturally brought into full play all my powers of observation and expression,
and so made this one of my gravest, and I think one of my most beautiful
busts. This work was unhurried and brooded over, and the drapery was
worked with great care. The lines, all running downwards like the rills of
a fountain, are essential to the effect of the bust, and help to express its
innermost meaning.' (From Jacob Epstein, *Let There Be Sculpture: An
Autobiography*, Michael Joseph, 1940, p. 116.)

Mark Gertler (1891–1939)

10
Self-Portrait, 1920
oil on canvas
42.5 x 29.2 cm
Arts Council Collection
© Estate of the artist 1998

The Jewish-born painter Mark Gertler was brought up in London's East End and studied at the Slade School of Art. Many of his meticulous early works are of members of his family, of the Jewish community in which he lived, and of friends such as the painter Dora Carrington.

By August 1920, Gertler had fifteen pictures ready for his first one-person exhibition at the Goupil Gallery, London, the following year. In April 1920 he had developed the first symptoms of tuberculosis. He wrote to Noel Carrington in May 1920: 'To pass away time, when there is no one to sit for me, I'm painting a small portrait of myself.' (From *Mark Gertler: Selected Letters*, edited by Noel Carrington.) In November 1920 he entered a sanatorium at Banchory near Aberdeen. He suffered from continued ill health and bouts of depression, and committed suicide in 1939.

Frank Dobson (1888–1963)

13
Portrait Bust of Lady Keynes (Lydia Lopokova), 1924
bronze
47 x 36 x 35 cm
Arts Council Collection
© Estate of the artist 1998

The sitter was the Russian-born dancer, Lydia Lopokova (1892–1981) who, as a member of Diaghilev's Ballets Russes, became known for her scintillating character-dancing in such works as *Petroushka*, *The Good-Humoured Ladies* and *La Boutique Fantasque*. During Diaghilev's London season of 1918–19 she came to know many members of the Bloomsbury Group and in 1925 she married the great economist John Maynard Keynes (later the first Chairman of the Arts Council of Great Britain). She was portrayed by many artists, including Picasso, Sickert, Duncan Grant, Vanessa Bell and Laura Knight. Keynes commissioned this bust of the dancer two years before their marriage. The sculpture was finished at the end of 1923, cost Keynes about £160 and was cast in bronze in 1924.

Stanley Spencer (1891–1959)

16
Self-Portrait, c.1926
pencil on paper
30.5 x 17.8 cm
Arts Council Collection

Spencer drew and painted himself throughout his life, usually as a single head or figure but occasionally with others such as in *The Leg of Mutton Nude* (1937, Tate Gallery) where he is seen naked with his wife Patricia Preece (cat. 21). His diminutive figure also appears in many of his religious and autobiographical compositions, most famously in *The Resurrection, Cookham* (1923–27, Tate Gallery).

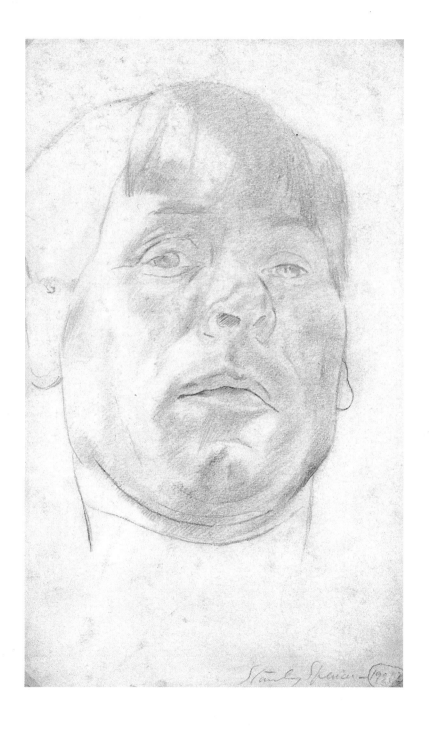

Ben Nicholson (1894–1982)

20
Crowned Head, The Queen, 1932
oil on canvas on board
91.5 x 120 cm
Abbot Hall Art Gallery, Kendal

This is almost certainly a portrait of Nicholson's second wife, the sculptor
Barbara Hepworth (1903–75), posed in front of their studio window at
St Ives in Cornwall. It is possible that the work was begun whilst Nicholson
was still living in Cumberland. Hepworth's distinctive profile appears in
several of Nicholson's works at this time such as the 1933 double portrait
of himself and her (National Portrait Gallery).

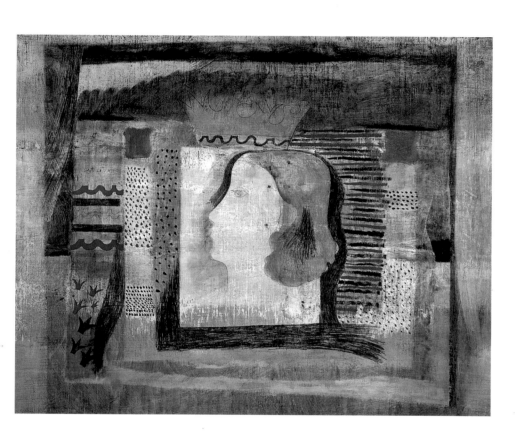

Stanley Spencer (1891–1959)

21
Nude Portrait of Patricia Preece, c.1935
oil on canvas
76.2 x 50.8 cm
Ferens Art Gallery, Hull

Shown at Ferens Art Gallery only

Patricia Preece (born Ruby Preece in 1894) was the artist's second wife and
this portrait dates from around the time of their marriage in 1937. Spencer's
best portraits are of himself, his friends and family, although on occasions
he accepted outside portrait commissions. Patricia Preece (who became
Lady Spencer and died in 1966) signed and exhibited works which in
fact were all painted for her by her long-term lover, Dorothy Hepworth
(1898–1978). This extraordinary story of devotion and deception only
became known after Dorothy Hepworth's death.

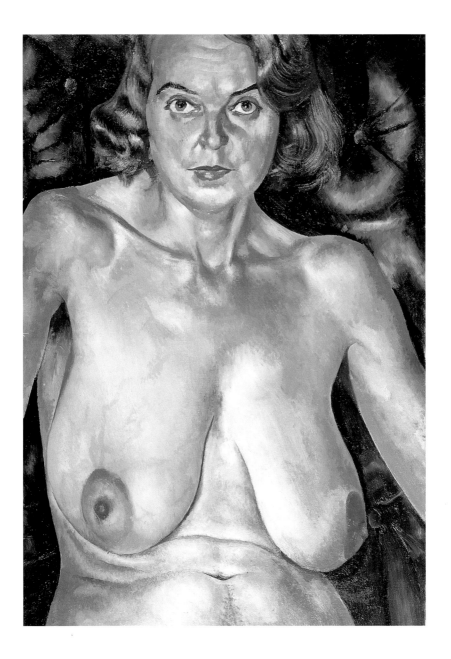

Robert Buhler (1916–89)

23
Stephen Spender, 1939
oil on canvas
75.5 x 62.8 cm
Victoria Art Gallery, Bath & North East Somerset
© Estate of the artist 1998
Shown at Victoria Art Gallery only

Stephen Spender (1909–95) was a poet and critic who, with Christopher Isherwood, W.H. Auden, C. Day Lewis and others, came to prominence in the 1930s. He fought with the Republicans in the Spanish Civil War and co-edited *Poems for Spain* (an anthology published in 1939, the year of Buhler's portrait) which reflect the political turmoil of the period. From 1939 to 1941 he was co-editor, with Cyril Connolly, of the monthly magazine *Horizon*. Spender was devoted to the visual arts, formed an extensive collection and was portrayed in paintings and drawings by Wyndham Lewis, Henry Moore, William Coldstream, Rodrigo Moynihan and David Hockney.

Robert Buhler is chiefly remembered as a landscape painter but he made outstanding portraits of friends such as Francis Bacon, Madge Garland and John Davenport.

Anthony Devas (1911–58)

24
Six O'Clock News, 1940
oil on canvas
50.8 x 76 cm
Arts Council Collection
© Estate of the artist 1998

The sitter in *Six O'Clock News* is the painter Rupert Shephard, who later married Nicolette Devas after the death of her first husband Anthony Devas, well known as a fashionable portraitist in the 1950s. Shephard described the painting of the picture in a letter to the Arts Council in 1985: 'It was painted at Walton-on-Thames, where for a short time Anthony and Nicolette shared a bungalow with me ... It was painted as dated 1940 and I was certainly listening, as we all did then somewhat apprehensively, to the wartime news at 6 o'clock.'

Lawrence Gowing (1918–91)

25
Julia Strachey, 1940
oil on canvas
75 x 62 cm
Arts Council Collection
© Estate of the artist 1998

The painter, teacher and writer on art, Lawrence Gowing met his first wife
Julia Strachey (1901–79) in 1938, lived with her from 1940 to 1948, and
married her in 1952 – the marriage was dissolved in 1967. This portrait
was painted in her London flat at 88 Charlotte Street and is one of several
portraits of her from the 1940s (including *Lady with Book*, Ashmolean
Museum, Oxford) which are among Gowing's finest works. Julia Strachey
was a niece of the writer Lytton Strachey and the author of short stories
and the novel *Cheerful Weather for the Wedding* (1932).

Bernard Meninsky (1891–1950)

27
Portrait of a Girl, 1942
oil on canvas
61 x 50.8 cm
Arts Council Collection

The identity of this serious young girl remains unknown but the work encapsulates Meninsky's frequently melancholy reading of his sitters. Like Mark Gertler, Meninsky committed suicide, depressed by the 'doubts and uncertainties' of his life and lack of recognition.

Vanessa Bell (1879–1961)

30
The Cook, 1948
oil on canvas
100.3 x 74.7 cm
Arts Council Collection
© Estate of the artist 1998

The model is Angelica (born 1918), Vanessa Bell's daughter by the painter
Duncan Grant. At this time Angelica was married to the writer David
Garnett and was the mother of four daughters. Vanessa Bell made many
portraits of her and introduced her into domestic scenes such as this.
The work was painted at the artist's home, Charleston in Sussex, a view
of the Downland landscape seen though the window (though no such
window exists at Charleston). For another portrait of Angelica Garnett
see cat. 33.

Josef Herman (b.1911)

31
The Welsh Miner, 1948
oil on board
78 x 58 cm
Arts Council Collection
© the artist 1998

The identity of the sitter is unknown but he was almost certainly a member of the Welsh mining community in which Josef Herman lived. Herman first visited the Welsh mining village of Ystradgynlais in 1944 and some years later he bought a dilapidated factory there which he and his wife transformed into a home and studio, living there for the next eleven years.

Francis Bacon (1909–92)

32
Head VI, 1949
oil on canvas
93.2 x 76.5 cm
Arts Council Collection
© Francis Bacon Estate 1998
Not shown at City Gallery, Leicester

Head VI was the last in Francis Bacon's group of male heads (1948–49) and the first of his celebrated series of paintings of Popes, loosely based on the portrait of Innocent X by Velázquez (Doria Gallery, Rome) which Bacon knew from reproduction rather than reality. The *Head* series formed the core of Bacon's first one-person show at the Hanover Gallery, London, in 1949. In one sense, the painting here is a variation on the theme of the Velázquez; in another, it embodies Bacon's personal anxieties and perhaps indirectly refers to his difficult past relations with his father (the Italian for Pope, of course, being 'Papa'). The open mouth may also relate, as has recently been suggested, to Bacon's chronic asthma which often left him prostrate, gasping for breath, his mouth, according to his sister, wide open.

Edward Le Bas (1904–66)

33
Angelica Garnett, 1950
oil on card
70.5 x 82.5 cm
Arts Council Collection
© Estate of the artist 1998

The painter and collector Edward Le Bas was a close friend and painting companion of the sitter's parents, Vanessa Bell and Duncan Grant. This portrait was painted in Le Bas' studio in Glebe Place, London. It is characteristic of his emphasis on giving his sitters a setting appropriate to their mood.

Angelica Garnett has had several exhibitions of her own work as a painter and she published a memoir, *Deceived with Kindness,* in 1984. She was painted by several artists, including Matthew Smith, and a portrait of her as a girl, playing a violin, by her father, is in Southampton City Art Gallery.

Lucian Freud (b.1922)

34
Girl in a Green Dress, 1954
oil on canvas
32.5 x 23.6 cm
Arts Council Collection
© the artist 1998

The model is the writer Lady Caroline Blackwood (1931–96). She married Lucian Freud in 1953 and sat for him for several early works (although she apparently disliked posing). A double portrait by Freud of himself and his wife, *Hotel Room* (1954), is in the Beaverbrook Art Gallery, Fredericton, New Brunswick. This close-up head is a fine example of Freud's early, forensic style.

Caroline Blackwood went on to marry the composer Israel Citkovitz, and later the American poet Robert Lowell. She wrote novels, short stories and *The Last Duchess* (1995), an alarming account of the Duchess of Windsor's final years.

Nigel Henderson (1917–85)

35
Head of a Man, 1956–61
oil and photographic processes on card
152.4 x 121.9 cm
Arts Council Collection
© Estate of the artist 1998

As a young man, Nigel Henderson met various members of the Bloomsbury Group and later married Virginia Woolf's niece, Judith Stephen. In 1938 he showed two collages at the Guggenheim Jeune in the company of Picasso, Braque and Gris. In the years prior to the Second World War, interested in both art and science, he took a job working for Dr Helmut Ruhemann, picture restorer at the National Gallery.

In 1945 Henderson enrolled as a student at the Slade School of Art, where he became friends with both Eduardo Paolozzi and Richard Hamilton. At the time there were no photographic facilities at the Slade, but after leaving he became increasingly interested in photography and began to experiment by drawing directly on to unexposed film. In 1956, as one of twelve groups to produce an environment, he, Paolozzi and the Smithsons created *Patio and Pavilion* for the Whitechapel Art Gallery exhibition *This is Tomorrow*. Part of Henderson's contribution to the project was *Head of a Man*, a photographic collage on paper mounted on board (Tate Gallery, London), which was derived from the same original negative of an initial collage as the Arts Council Collection's *Head of a Man*, although the latter was worked up further in oil paint rather than in collage.

Richard Hamilton (b.1922)

37
Portrait of Hugh Gaitskell as a Famous Monster of Filmland, 1964
oil and photomontage on panel
61 x 61 cm
Arts Council Collection

When this painting was conceived, Hugh Gaitskell (1906–63) was Leader of the Labour Party, and Richard Hamilton regarded him as a 'political monster' because of his vacillation over forming a clear anti-nuclear policy for his Party. In the portrait, Gaitskell's features, taken from a newspaper photograph, are fused with those of a fictional monster (the actor Claude Rains made up as the Phantom of the Opera) as seen on the cover of a contemporary magazine called *Famous Monsters of Filmland* (issue 10). By the time the work was finished, Gaitskell had died, adding an unexpected *frisson* to Hamilton's biting image.

Frank Auerbach (b.1931)

38
J.Y.M. in the Studio VII, 1965
oil on board
92.5 x 44.5 cm
On loan to Abbot Hall Art Gallery, Kendal
© the artist 1998
Shown at Abbot Hall Art Gallery only

Frank Auerbach's long series of portraits of J.Y.M. began in about 1964.
Throughout his career, Auerbach has used primarily two models, J.Y.M. and
E.O.W., painted and drawn repeatedly in his Camden Town studio. Other
sitters have included Catherine Lampert, Director of the Whitechapel Art
Gallery, and David Landau, editor of *Print Quarterly*. On painting people,
Auerbach has commented: '... if one has a chance of seeing people apart
from the time when one's painting them, one notices all sorts of things
about them. If one sees them in movement, one realises all sorts of truths
about them and one's infinitely less likely to be satisfied with a superficial
statement.' (From *Frank Auerbach*, exhibition catalogue, Arts Council of
Great Britain, 1978.)

David Hockney (b.1937)

39
Portrait Surrounded by Artistic Devices, 1965
acrylic and collage on canvas
152.4 x 182.9 cm
Arts Council Collection
© David Hockney 1965

The sitter is the artist's father, Kenneth Hockney, surrounded by 'images
and elements of [Hockney's] and other artists' work and ideas of the time'.
In an implied criticism of Modernism, Hockney has juxtaposed a 'realistic'
portrait of a loved parent (closely based on a drawing of his father made
from life) with motifs inspired by Cézanne (cylinders and cones) and
contemporary abstraction. He seems to suggest that the 'human' element
of all aesthetic endeavour should not be overwhelmed by close adherence
to theory. The outcome of such criticism is apparent in Hockney's double
portrait of his parents (1977) in the Tate Gallery.

Howard Hodgkin (b.1932)

40
Mrs K, 1966–67
oil on canvas
86.4 x 99 cm
Arts Council Collection
© the artist 1998

The title refers to Jane Kasmin, wife of the art dealer John Kasmin, whose gallery in London in the 1960s and 1970s was a showcase for work by many of the best known British and American artists of the period. In his monograph on Hodgkin (1994), Andrew Graham-Dixon writes that Jane Kasmin 'is recalled, in paint, as a solitary ghost, a blur of flesh and bright candy-coloured clothes occluded by a blue void ... The painting belongs within a tradition of female portraits whose themes are aloneness and vulnerability ...'

Michael Andrews (1928–96)

41
Study of a head for a group of figures No. 6, 1967
oil on board
22 x 15 cm
Arts Council Collection
© Estate of the artist 1998

This was a preparatory study for a large group portrait, *The Lord Mayor's Reception in Norwich Castle Keep on the eve of the installation of the first Chancellor of the University of East Anglia* (1966–69), which was commissioned from Michael Andrews in 1965 by the Museums Committee of the Castle Museum, Norwich. Andrews was attracted by the idea that the gathering would not be exclusive but typical of the whole community in which he had been brought up. To record the event he employed a local photographer and, from his photographs, Andrews made a collage. For the final seven-foot square picture, Nigel Henderson (cat. 35) devised a method for projecting and printing the collage on to Turaphot linen and did this for him. After the linen was stuck to the canvas, Andrews proceeded with painting.

This preparatory sketch was torn up and discarded by Andrews, but the artist Colin Self retrieved it, pasted it together and convinced him to use it.

David Hockney (b.1937)

42
Study for Portrait of Christopher Isherwood and Don Bachardy, 1968
watercolour on paper
48.2 x 60.2 cm
Arts Council Collection
© David Hockney 1968

The novelist Christopher Isherwood (1904–86) was educated at Repton
School and at Corpus Christi, Cambridge, and taught English in Germany
from 1930 to 1933. His best known novels, *Mr Norris Changes Trains* (1935)
and *Goodbye to Berlin* (1939), were based on his experiences of pre-Hitler
Berlin and later inspired John Van Druten's play *I Am a Camera* which was
turned into the musical *Cabaret*. He emigrated to California to work as a
Hollywood scriptwriter in 1939, and became a US citizen in 1946. David
Hockney admired Isherwood as an author and, when he was their
neighbour in California, became a close friend of Isherwood and his
boyfriend, the artist Don Bachardy. The setting for this double portrait
is Isherwood's living room in his home at 145 Adelaide Drive, Santa
Monica. Hockney took innumerable photographs of his sitters, made
this compositional sketch and some pencil drawings and finished the oil
painting in 1968.

Gilbert & George (b.1943, b.1942)

43
Still from *A Portrait of The Artists as Young Men*, 1972
black and white video tape recording and framed certificate
8 minutes duration
Arts Council Collection
© the artists 1998

The artists Gilbert and George met in 1967 when they were both studying sculpture at St Martin's School of Art and their first collaborative works date from 1968. They became known for their singing sculpture *Underneath the Arches* and first worked with video in 1970. Two years later they agreed to make three further video works for the Düsseldorf gallery owner Gerry Schum. One of the three was *A Portrait of The Artists as Young Men* (the other two were *In the Bush* and *Gordon's Makes us Drunk*). For *A Portrait of The Artists as Young Men* the sound track of thunder and rain was taken from a sound effects record which was bought especially for the purpose. ' "Thunder is a very emotional sound for the sculptors." As for the title, it was chosen, they said, "just in terms of the nerves!" and continued: "We're so interested in portraiture. It's all one big portrait." ' (From *The Tate Gallery 1972–74 Biennial Report and Illustrated Catalogue of Acquisitions*.)

Maggi Hambling (b.1945)

45
Frances Rose (4), 1975
oil on canvas
57.9 x 52.9 cm
Arts Council Collection
© the artist 1998

The sitter was an elderly neighbour whom Hambling began to paint in 1973. Unlike three earlier portraits of the same model, the present version was done from memory. Throughout her career, Hambling has alternated imaginative works and landscape with an extensive series of portraits and self-portraits. Notably, she has painted the comedian Max Wall and the scientist Dorothy Hodgkin, and has recently been engaged on a memorial sculpture to Oscar Wilde.

Leon Kossoff (b.1926)

46
Portrait of George Thompson, 1975
oil on board
123 x 78 cm
Arts Council Collection
© the artist 1998

Leon Kossoff has described George Thompson simply as 'a friend of the artist'. Like Lucian Freud and Frank Auerbach, Kossoff usually paints only members of his family and close friends. Capturing a likeness of his sitters seems to be less important to him than considerations of mood and atmosphere.

Keith Arnatt (b.1930)

47
from *The Visitors* series, 1976–77
silver bromide photograph
series of 28 photographs, each 25 x 25 cm
Arts Council Collection
© the artist 1998

The Visitors series of 28 portraits of visitors to Tintern Abbey (1975–76)
was one of three sets of portraits made by Keith Arnatt between 1975 and
1979 (the others were *Walking the Dog* and *Gardeners*). 'Initially, Arnatt
emphasized the parallel between his way of working and the "naive"
directness of the snapshot. Writing of [*The Visitors*]... he commented,
"I think of them as pseudo-snapshots." ' (From *Keith Arnatt: Rubbish and
Recollections*, exhibition catalogue, Photographers' Gallery, London and
Oriel Mostyn, 1989, p. 17.)

Tony Bevan (b.1951)

49
Portrait of a Martyr, 1982
dry pigment, PVA and charcoal on Triwall
190 x 114 cm
Arts Council Collection
© the artist 1998

This is not a portrait of a specific person. As its title suggests, the work
is intended symbolically. Of such works, Tony Bevan commented: 'I am
interested in showing an individual reflecting the state of society that
conditions our present. I usually paint a person from a combination of
memory and photographs. Not photographs of that person, but
photographs that might relate to the composition of the picture. Very
often the person depicted in the picture doesn't appear to look like the
person who was initially the subject of the painting.' (From *Before it hits
the floor*, exhibition catalogue, ICA, London, 1982.)

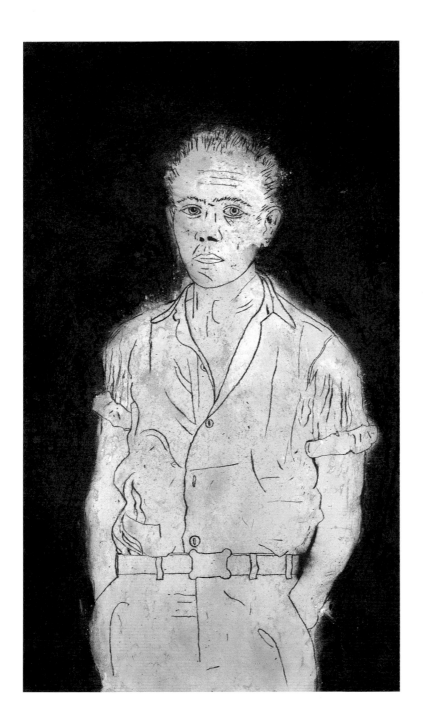

John Coplans (b.1920)

50
Self-Portrait (Upside down no. 1), 1992
silver gelatin print, edition 2 of 6
220 x 114.5 cm
Arts Council Collection
© the artist 1998

The photographer and writer on art John Coplans began experimenting with photography in his late 50s, taking photographs of his naked body. His first group of photographs to be published was *A Body of Work* in 1987.

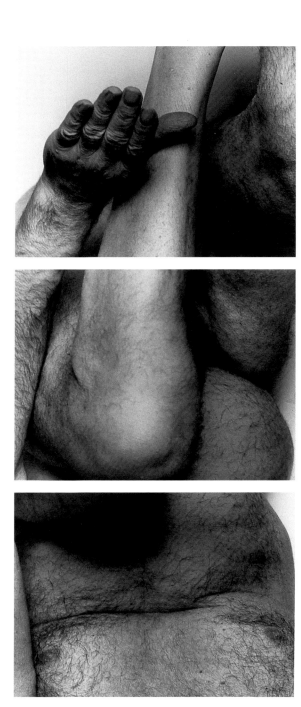

Richard Billingham (b.1970)

51
Untitled, 1995
SFA4 colour photograph mounted on aluminium
50 x 75 cm
Arts Council Collection
© the artist 1998

This is a photograph of the artist's mother, Elizabeth (born 1950), and is one of a series of pictures taken of Billingham's family. He has made the following statement about these pictures: 'I started using a camera about six years ago. I felt I needed some kind of reference material for my paintings as it is quite difficult to get people to give their time to pose for you. I was still living with my dad at the time, Liz wasn't living with us then; she had left due to Ray's incessant drinking and moaning. She seldom visited. This was all quite sad and I wanted to make paintings about it that were very moving: that would express the tragedy of it all. When I printed up the photographs (I worked in black and white then because it was cheaper than colour) I was apprehensive about letting on to anybody about who they were of for fear of becoming unpopular with the other students who were, I believe, all from much more financially and spiritually secure family backgrounds. I was fairly introvert as a teenager because I had always been somewhat embarrassed about the "state" of my family. Yet after a few months at college I realised that by letting students and, especially, tutors know who the paintings and photographs were really of I could come clean about the family history and relate to people naturally. This was quite a load off me and since then I think I've been taking pictures of my close family not just as a reference for paintings but also as an attempt to comprehend myself and them more fully ... It is certainly not my intention to shock, to offend, to sensationalize, be political or whatever. Only to make work that is as spiritually meaningful as I can make it. Whatever the medium.'
(From *Camera Austria International*, N55, 1996, p. 4.)

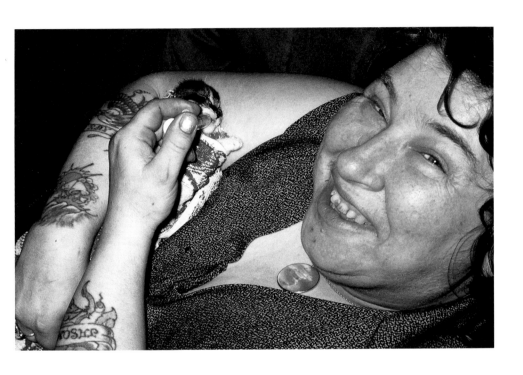

Victoria Hall (b.1972)

52
Family Tree Part I (detail) and *Family Tree Part II*, 1995
acetate, photographs and text
dimensions variable
Arts Council Collection
© the artist 1998
Not shown at City Gallery, Leicester

Victoria Hall described *Family Tree* in an artist's statement accompanying
her application to EAST International 1995 (EAST International is an open
exhibition held annually): 'The two installations present a system that is
commonly recognized, yet the information that is shown within is surprising
for the viewer, thus enabling the work to hold the viewer's attention. It
represents the way in which families often treat the other members, such
as when someone has died they are remembered for one incident alone,
or when one has gained a reputation for a particular reason. A strong point
of the work is that it is not so much a particular family but a formula that
could be applied to any family – thus the viewer can relate to the work with
the individual knowledge, interests and background that they bring with
them to the work.'

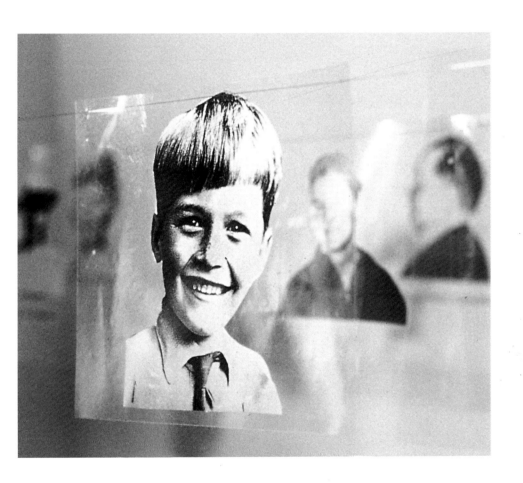

Richard Patterson (b.1963)

53
Self-Portrait, 1996
oil on canvas
147.3 x 111.8 cm
Southampton City Art Gallery
© the artist, courtesy of Anthony d'Offay Gallery, London
Shown at Southampton City Art Gallery and Abbot Hall Art Gallery only

Of this work, Richard Patterson has recently said: 'I was in Vienna, helping install Simon [Patterson]'s *J.P.233 in C.S.O. Blue* wall drawing for the *Doubletake* show. Aldo Rossi, the architect, did the interiors for the show, and had made an interior space within an interior space. It seemed to be done in a very po-faced way, and there were all these po-faced curators with strange rectilinear glasses. So I made these "Philosopher's Glasses" with Wittgenstein on the side where you might have Armani or whatever. And then we took a photograph of me in a pseudo-architect pose, with the installation plan of Simon's work. The shape behind me was a window, which gave it a kind of de Chirico quality. The photograph was taken from above, and then the painting of the photograph was done from below, so you get an effect of convergence, false perspective, which again is de Chirico. That interested me.'(From *Paintings by Richard Patterson*, exhibition catalogue, Anthony d'Offay Gallery, 1997.)

Richard Hamilton (b.1922)

54
Portrait of Derek Jarman, 1996–97
digital colour transfer print
39.4 x 39.4 cm
Arts Council Collection

Portrait of Derek Jarman is one of 40 colour pigment transfer prints, all taken from an original portrait by Hamilton of the film maker, artist and writer Derek Jarman, painted just before he died from AIDS.

Works not illustrated

2 **Walter Richard Sickert** (1860–1942)
The Juvenile Lead, 1907
oil on canvas, 51 x 45.8 cm
Southampton City Art Gallery
Shown at Southampton City Art Gallery and
Abbot Hall Art Gallery only

3 **Alfred Wolmark** (1877–1961)
Self-Portrait, 1910
oil on canvas, 76.8 x 64.1 cm
Southampton City Art Gallery
Shown at Southampton City Art Gallery and
Abbot Hall Art Gallery only

5 **Henri Gaudier-Brzeska** (1891–1915)
Self-Portrait, 1912
bronze (cast in 1939, 1 of 7 casts)
17 x 16 x 18.5 cm
New Walk Museum, Leicester City Museums
Shown at City Gallery, Leicester, only

6 **Henri Gaudier-Brzeska** (1891–1915)
Bust of Alfred Wolmark, 1913
bronze, height 66.7 cm
Southampton City Art Gallery
Shown at Southampton City Art Gallery and
Abbot Hall Art Gallery only

11 **Percy Wyndham Lewis** (1882–1957)
Mr Wyndham Lewis as a Tyro, c.1920/21
oil on canvas, 75.5 x 45 cm
Ferens Art Gallery, Hull
Shown at Abbot Hall Art Gallery and
Ferens Art Gallery only

12 **Ambrose McEvoy** (1878–1927)
Mrs Claude Johnson in Black, 1922
oil on canvas, 127 x 101.6 cm
Ferens Art Gallery, Hull
Shown at Ferens Art Gallery only

14 **Gilbert Spencer** (1892–1979)
Garsington Youth, 1925
oil on canvas, 94.7 x 75.1 cm
Victoria Art Gallery, Bath & North East Somerset
Shown at Victoria Art Gallery only

15 **Mark Gertler** (1891–1939)
Marjorie Gertler, c.1925
pastel on paper, 68.3 x 88.4 cm
Abbot Hall Art Gallery, Kendal
Shown at Abbot Hall Art Gallery only

17 **Victor Pasmore** (b.1908)
Seated Figure, the Maid: Florence Head, 1927–28
oil on panel, 46.3 x 39.5 cm
Abbot Hall Art Gallery, Kendal
Shown at Abbot Hall Art Gallery only

18 **Barbara Hepworth** (1903–75)
Head, 1930
Cumberland stone, 28 x 17 x 40 cm
New Walk Museum, Leicester City Museums
Shown at City Gallery, Leicester, only

19 **Glyn W. Philpot** (1884–1937)
Frank Mundy Coombs, undated (probably 1930–37)
oil on canvas, 55 x 38 cm
Victoria Art Gallery, Bath & North East Somerset
Shown at Victoria Art Gallery only

22 **Meredith Frampton** (1894–1984)
A Game of Patience, 1937
oil on canvas, 106.7 x 78.7 cm
Ferens Art Gallery, Hull
Shown at Ferens Art Gallery only

26 **Victor Pasmore** (b.1908)
Portrait of a Girl, 1941
oil on canvas, 61 x 50.8 cm
Arts Council Collection

28 **David Bomberg** (1890–1957)
Portrait of Jimmy Newmark, 1943
oil on canvas, 76.2 x 65.3 cm
Abbot Hall Art Gallery, Kendal
Shown.at Abbot Hall Art Gallery only

29 **Kurt Schwitters** (1887–1948)
Portrait of Mr Routledge, 1945
oil on canvas, 70 x 54 cm
Abbot Hall Art Gallery, Kendal
Shown at Abbot Hall Art Gallery only

36 **David Hockney** (b.1937)
Life Painting for Myself, 1962
oil on canvas, 122 x 91.4 cm
Ferens Art Gallery, Hull
Shown at Ferens Art Gallery only

44 **Michael Craig-Martin** (b.1941)
Kid's Stuff 1–7, 1973
mirror, tape and text on plastic
7 pieces, each 40.6 x 30.5 cm
Arts Council Collection

48 **Peter Greenham** (1909–92)
*Portrait of an Old Woman (Charlotte,
Lady Bonham-Carter)*, 1981
oil on canvas, 91.2 x 61.4 cm
Southampton City Art Gallery
Shown at Southampton City Art Gallery and
Abbot Hall Art Gallery only